Compulsions and Other Habits

By Daisy-Ella

This is my poetry diary.

It wasnt ever intended to be for other people but after sharing a poem with a few close friends I was convinced to post them online and then over time I decided to write a book of them...

This is the first part of my series of poetry books, just to test the waters a little.

I hope you enjoy it

A note from the Author

Hello, dear reader! My name is Daisy-Ella and I guess Im now a writer! Wow that's weird to say... Before this I was pretty much nobody, just some sort of mess that people generally steered clear of, but since discovering writing a few years ago I have become bolder, brighter and on the whole a better person.

I have come to terms with my struggles with borderline personality disorder, obsessive compulsive disorder, complex-PTSD and bulimia (just to name a few) and I have reduced my self-harm. How have I done this? Therapy. Whether that's from a professional therapist or whether that's self help through writing and poetry, it has helped me. So I hope you enjoy reading through my deepest thoughts and learning about what its like to be me...

Disclaimer; these are my thoughts, my feelings. You may not agree with me but please respect this this is how I feel about my current situation and poetry has helped me come to terms with how Ive been feeling for so many years. Thank you.

Rape is Not a Dirty Word

They teach you not to speak,
But I cannot hide away,
Because the statistics will remind us,
800 get raped per day.
That's one every 107 seconds,
How many people do you know?!
For one in five girls will be assaulted,
Internal scars don't show.
The stigma is still around us,
"I wonder what she wore?"
That 6 year old was exploited,
You think that she's a "whore"?!
If we're going to make a difference,
It starts with knowing facts,
If it was about what she was wearing,
Girls wouldn't get raped in slacks.
Men get attacked too,
It doesn't make them gay!
Rapists attack anyone,

Yet only 2% are locked away.

An abusers main motive

Is to manipulate you're life,

If it was about sex,

Men wouldn't rape their wives.

This is not about myself,

It's about kids younger than four,

That can't let people know,

What's happening behind doors.

So speak up if you were raped,

There's no need to be afraid!!

They cannot get you now,

You're no longer in their shade.

Be accepting of survivors,

And hear the word they speak,

Being raped will not break them,

And don't ever call them weak.

Remember what I've told you,

Be the change you want to see,

If people knew this ten years ago,

It might not have happened to me

Insignificant

I was insignificant
A small fish in a big pond
One single leaf on the tree of life that's swirling and
blowing in the wind, holding on for dear life but I
couldn't keep my grip and I fell into the chasm of
darkness and despair where no one could reach me and
I was lost
I was a leaf
Stuck in a puddle
Gasping for air after each submerged moment where I
was trod into the water by the people I was told to look
up to because they might just pick me or call me
beautiful and treasure me
I was a leaf
A single leaf
A lonely, dying leaf away from my branch that supplied
me with life and I did nothing. I gazed to the tree where
I should've stayed but the pressure of gravities pull
became too much just like society's oppression and the
standards we must meet to become "normal"
I don't want to be normal
My life in the puddle is lonely
And can be cold
And you know what?; this isn't how I imagined things
But I know other leaves have fallen

And they survived
And they weren't insignificant anymore
And one day
More will join me

I need order…

How do I feel?
I don't know
I don't think there's even a word.....
Desperate?
Lost?
Alone?
More like I'm desperately lost on the journey to not be
alone
Because when I'm alone the pain hits
And I don't have the armour to protect myself from the
feelings that eat up my bones from the inside
Things have to be in order
Things have to be checked
Because if I don't check them I'm not in control and I'm
not in control what am I?
There isn't a word for what I'm feeling.
There isn't a word to protect me from the lack of order
in my life.....
That's why I need to be in control and have order
because the lack of order sticks to me like the leaves
you found in the grass when we were children
It was fun to stick them on others but not fun to peel of
ourselves
The world is out of order and disorganised and has no
pattern and yes it keeps spinning and spinning and

spinning and spinning like there's nothing wrong but
there is!
I need to find order
I need to have control
I need a word to tell you how I'm feeling
And
-there isn't one

Contradiction

There's never been a more contradicting statement than
the one I say to myself most days;
"I want to die"
See, the ability to die is a privilege and why should that
privilege be awarded to me when I have barely lived
enough to know that it is what I truly want.
So many people have asked to live long lives when here
I am wanting the opposite and why can't I trade places
with the ones who have died too young? Why can't I?
It would only do good.
The irony of wanting anything is such a mind fuck. I
only know I want to be cold when I'm overheating. I
only know I want food because I am hungry. I only
know I want to die because I am alive! I am alive! And
I will stay this way because this is the only way to keep
the sadness and the sadness is familiar like the old
clothes of my late grandfather; the memory of the smell
is not a joyful one but it is the only thing I know.
Too many people have been lost too young and I will
not be one of them, I will keep going and I will not be
the person people mourn unless tragedy strikes but deep
down I do not want the tragedy for I am not a play, I do
not want the impact of the car against my chest as I am
not the barrier when the driver has slipped off the road.
I am a human, not a statistic of suicide. I am a person,

not a book to finish. ...
I am a contradiction

Why is it appealing?

All these lies coming from your lips…

What do they taste like?

Do they taste like the bitter peel of a lemon or are they sugary and sweet to you?

Do they glide out of your mouth in one swift motion or are they rocks and sand that you spit on the floor because the grittiness is too hard to deal with?

Will they ever stop or is this an eternal wound, gushing blood like a river and only stopping to crash into whatever's in front of you?

Why do you do it?

Why is my life of pain something you strive to have and why is it something you feel you must replicate in your own life when it's the mirror image of hell itself?

Your lies affect me in the deepest way.

The anger it stirs is like a cut to my chest I cant ever get control of and I know I will bleed out eventually if I cant get a grasp on the artery and staunch the blood.

It will fill up the gaps between my organs until there's no space for my lungs or stomach to expand with the nutrients I need to maintain my soul.

Please, for the love of Buddah, stop lying about things that affect every moment of my life.

I don't understand why you do it…

What the fuck is so appealing about my pain?

Threats

Threats
Of what?
Death?!
Why should I fear death when for seven years I've been
chasing him asking him to turn and face me and take
my soul to whichever afterlife I belong in?
Why should death scare me when it's the only thing life
can guarantee to end with?
Why is it scaring me to my core when I have crossed
the line twice before
More threats
Of what?
Hell?!
With this illness, baby, I'm already there. Checking and
checking and locking and locking and safety and safety
and stay alive, stay alive!
Why would hell be any more painful than a check of L
O C K E D "locked" every five minutes when my head
is tired, my hands are sweating and my legs are folding
beneath me?
There is nothing that should scare me....
And yet when those threats are aimed as another life I
will check I will check I will lock I will lock and keep
safe and keep safe and keep them alive, keep alive....
Compulsions, I'm not scared of what you will do to

me....
But please, don't hurt my loved ones

Bulimic Teeth

The inside of her mouth was like the inside of her mind

Holes within the structure that not even love could bind

Pasty light white muscle- strong but wearing thin

Give it one more push and break down could begin

Her vocal chords are rusted like the space inside her skull

They're important to survive with, but maintaining can be dull

For what's the point in treating the physical signs of waste

When tomorrow for the hundredth time she'll get that acid taste

So chipped and frayed her mouth might be but that'll have to be okay

For dentists can but fix your teeth- not show your mind the way

Bright Colours

Tweezers in one hand and my thoughts in the other
Why am I doing this?
What will I accomplish from pulling my toenails out?
Obviously the answer is nothing but somehow I can't
help but do it and why?
Because my brain turns red...
Or bright blue...
Or orange!
A bright and uncomfortable colour that I can't sit with
and the only way to go back to the normal shade that
means I can function is to do this horrible thing.
I don't enjoy it.
But I don't enjoy a lot of things I have to do.
This disorder, so they tell me, is called dermatillomania
which is the urge to pick at your skin or nails
But not in the same way a fourteen year old bites the
loose skin around their fingers but in the way a butcher
slices his meat for market
This is not something I enjoy but something I have to
do.
Because, brains aren't meant to be bright colours....
They're meant to be functioning.
And I am not right now

Within YOU

Do you want me to inspire you into doing the things you are unable to do?
Sweetheart, that strength is not something I can manufacture in your soul. The change has to come from within and it's something you have to create.
I am not able to change your mind about the way your emotions manifest but I will give my all to supporting you when you aren't feeling your greatest.
Drown yourself in sorrows
If that makes you feel better
But tomorrow will come and you have to see yourself in a brighter, sharper spot-light because I am not in your life's production team but merely an audience member cheering you on from the crowd.
I cannot change your mind, your thoughts are your own to steer into a better corner where the sun can reach and the plants will grow and the planets will turn.
The sunlight is where I see you.
But where do you see yourself?

<u>Dear Mental Illnesses,</u>

Tonight, I am going to address you as one, because despite being separate knives ready to stab me in the throat when Im least expecting it- you do all come from the same cutlery drawer. So here goes;

You. You have robbed me of so much. You have taken years from me where I could've started to repair the damage that was done. You have taken so many chances of finding happiness again and I wont let you take another. This time, the goal is in sight and I feel like I might make it out of this dark hole that *you* put me in.

This is the first time in years I have felt this optimistic and that is because of you. You stole my optimism, something that I have previously had in abundance, but now sit with only a few shreds of hope on my knees. That is because of you, I know this because as I am slowly beating you, I am finding more and more slithers of hope landing in my hands- and one day I will have enough to top up my glass, which will always be half **full.**

You once told me I was fat. Do you know how many years I spent trying to please you and make you say I was small enough? No?! Of course you dont, because that would mean you would actually have to pay attention to me. Its funny how I put all this effort into pleasing and satisfying you when youve never given a damn about me. You never even looked long enough to know if I was fat or not.... You just said it to torture me.

I wish I had the strength years ago to push past you and never let you get so ingrained in me. I wish you never made a dent in my soul, never mind the cuts on my arms made at your command. I could be scar-less, does that occur to you? I could have bare arms, none of these marks that people say make me stronger. That in itself is a lie. My scars dont make me strong... I would be just as strong with out them. They are just another addition that *you* made to my body without thought for me.

If you were a person youd be a man, youd be taller than me and youd appear to be stronger, but your muscles would be a facade. You would be weak inside, putting on this front so that you could 'prove yourself' to be something youre not. None the less- that facade would work on me. I would be, and have been, frightened and powerless (or so I thought) to you. I would be drawn to you and cherish the charisma, the appeal that got me to believe that if I went by your rules, things would be alright. That maybe you would help me. Oh how was I wrong.

There have been many times Ive tried to shut you out for good- but Ive never been able to because part of me--- part of me still clings to you. Its not a part of me I like, nor a part of me I am able to command- but none the less, its still me.

I wonder if youll ever leave. Because other than that one tiny grasp that says it still wants you because youre familiar, youre the norm, youve been within my life for so long---- other than that part that still wants you, I am ready to let go- more than that. I am ready to actively push you away. Away from my hopes and my dreams. Away from my family that long for me to be safe. Away from those tiny hands clinging to your shirt because it smells like home. Im ready to be away from you.

You.
Are.
Toxic to me.

Dear Mental Illness.... I want to break up.

"Just like a firework" she said,
"Im gonna go up in flames."

Im losing.

Not that life was ever a game you understand. Its as though my life has become a game because its competitors, you and I, have challenged it to do so. We spend our lives trying to make our bodies the best and our IQ scores the highest and our pay-cheques the biggest. Not only is my body, IQ and pay-cheque completely unsatisfactory. but I am losing at so many other aspects of life.

I dont have the energy to resit this exam. I dont have the energy to do anything at this point. I dont even have the energy to fully explains why I have equated life to an exam, test or trial.

I just have nothing left. And Im depressed by it. Because I want to go back in time to when I was 12 years old and tell someone what was going on in that moment and I just cant do that. I cant change what has happened and Im at a loss as to how I move forward from it.

I feel like Im going to be unwell forever and I dont like the idea of that. I dont like the idea of it at all. But I cant take myself out of the game. Im not a quitter. So I am in this state of instability and ambivalence and Im fed up of it.

No doubt Ill feel better in the morning, so I shall make a cup of tea and I will try and sleep this mood off because its exhausting me. I just needed to ramble for a bit. But Im done now.

You know youre a bereaved mother when

When you can't appreciate Christmas because your baby should be there. When a pregnant woman or mother and child makes you ache. When you baby sit someone's child and you get told "you're so good with kids! You should have one, one-day!" and it feels like a punch in the throat.

When you can't love anything or anyone anywhere close to the amount you love that child- and people don't understand it.

Life isn't fun, and you can't let it be. Because every time you enjoy yourself you feel like you shouldn't because your baby isn't with you and having fun makes you feel like a bad parent. And if you ever do let go and have fun you will see a swing set or a baby in a pram or a lady with a bump or an advertisement aimed at children and the memories are too much so you end up feeling such a mess because that joy should be shared with your child.

When every time someone dies, you think of how their mother must be feeling.

When someone is smoking or drinking while pregnant and you want to scream and tell them what they are risking.

When people can't understand why you're crying over your period so much or getting angry about someone going near a wooden box on your shelf because little do they know- that box has little reminders of your tiny angel.

When you get looked at weirdly for carrying your dog/cat/pet/teddy like a baby but it's the only way you can feel the sensation that you crave- too be depended on.

When someone tells you "I know how you feel" when they don't it's painful enough. But imagine losing a part of you and then someone saying "I know how you feel- my dog died last year" after you tell them your child is dead, it's an anger like you can't even fathom. So this is for a little in site into my every day life.

I am always going to be Marco's mum and I'm always going to be torn in two by his death. And I will talk about it as much as I damn please...

Body and Mind

"Please stop"

I would if I could body, but it's harder than that. "But it's hurting me"

And you don't think it's hurting me? To be filled with all this sadness and to hurt you so much?

"When will it stop?"

I don't know. I hope soon. I can't keep going much longer. "Don't make us die, why can't you get better rather than kill us"

YOU DONT GET IT ITS NOT A FUCKING CHOICE

"Yes, it is Dee. Say no to bulimia and say yes to treating me right"

Body, if I knew how- I would. But you don't know what it's like to be a mind filed with different personalities and voices and to be plagued by mental illness. You don't understand the pain of being forced to do things you dont what to do!!!

"But that's what you are doing to me!"

You know the physical side of being controlled- not the mental ache of being possessed by this evil being that personifies my pain. We are two different beings and we may never get along... But I will do my best to treat you right along our path together

The fat anorexic

You fed my body but you never helped my mind!

You thought if maybe I gained weight, that you would *surely* find,

That anorexia would disappear and become a pre-teen phase,

Like the bubble gum, the fizzy drinks and the dope I blazed.

But feeding me did nothing good, if anything it made me worse,

For I became transfixed on putting my "fat" body in a hearse.

Because you fixed my broken frame but never let me talk,

And now when I explain my pain, the doctors laugh and squawk!

So I developed a new method, one I thought might help me cope,

But bulimia, "the fat girls diet", is more numbing than the dope.

Bulimia could kill me, although the doctors say,

That my weight is high enough to end in a heart attack one day.

All because you never taught me anything about nourishing my soul,

But you were strict as hell on rules like scraping out my bowl.

And now they will not help me, because of my BMI,

And who would treat the fat girl when a skinny girl could die?

It's not right! It's not fair! Don't you see what you have done?!

You've given me the bullets for me to fill my gun.

You made the anorexic fat without helping fix her thoughts,

And all I ever asked for was to patiently be taught,

About how calories are numbers- they don't define your worth,

They cannot give you the importance of you staying on this earth

So my body now is overweight, and my brain a fragile vase

But hey, I guess it's fine now that there's fat upon my face.

Please help me learn to be okay- it's not wrong for me to ask!

And since when was beating my ED going to be an easy task.

Just let me learn and I will engage, but I need your help to grow!

Because I have no idea which the right way is to go.

Take away my pain
Theres nothing I can gain
From going against the grain
But my faith will stay the same

Marco-Zachary Oliver

Maybe I can change what

Actually happened

Re-write the

Chain of events

Of the most painful night of my life

Zoo days for your birthday

Admiring the way you

Change as you grow

Helping you do the things you cant

Accomplish yet and

Reading to you at night. I might just

Realise what ive been missing all these

Years Ive lived without you

Oh the fun we would have

Living like we should

I'd never take anything for granted and Id

Veer towards taking more chances, doing

Everything Ive ever wanted, but

Really, all I want… is you.

Relapse

Relapse
Even the word is appealing
The soft start and the crisp ending
Re
La
Pse
...
Maybe if I do it I will feel better
Maybe I will have a purpose
Because doing this to myself has been my world for so
long that I don't know what I'm doing if I'm not self
harming
Or dying
I'd love to be dying
Exploding blood vessels in my eyes
Popping my neck out of joint
This is my dream
But the reality is that my worst days in recovery are so
much better than my best days in relapse
I know I can beat this
I know it's possible
But the other option is so fucking appealing

Angry

I'm angry
But I don't know why
But EVERYTHING is making me angry
I see something sweet and it's sickly
I see something cute and it's cloying
Everything is making me angry
And I just want to relax but
I can't
Because life is the prize cunt that's pissed on my parade
Even though
In reality
Nothing bad is happening now
My parade is still marching on
But I'm still angry.

Infinity can be a feeling

Infinity can be a feeling.
Like the infinite love you give to your partner when
they have your heart and hold it between their fingers
delicately and swirl it around like it will keep the evil
away because my love WILL protect her
It'll do it's damn best
It will encompass her and support her
It will hold her own love in its arms
It will be there forever
THAT is infinity

Get me out

Get me out
I didn't ask for this
Get me out
I didn't dream of this
Get me the fuck out
This is not what I asked for
Get me out
This is not what I signed up for
Get me out
Of this pit I'm in
Get me out
Of this trap I've been trapped in
Get me the hell out
I isn't what I thought would happen
Get me OUT!!!
This is not what I wanted to happen
Get me out
I didn't ask for this
Get me out
I didn't dream of this

The tale of the missing toe nail

This is the tale of the missing toe nail
He was picked and was pulled fully off
It wasn't much fun
But it had to be done
Same as clearing your throat with a cough
-

There's no logical way to explain why all his remains
Were thrown in the bin without thought
Skin picking disorder
Has no fucking order
Even with coping skills I've been taught
-

I wish I could keep him, not pull him and cheat him
Away from the growth he had left
So much he could grow
On my short stubby toe
If I hadn't have tugged him to death
-

Now my toe is so sore, and bloody and raw
Like a shell-less cold, ugly snail
I hope you pardon my rhyme
For this was the time
For the tail of the missing toe nail

Darling, Dorothy

How I hate to see you in pain, throwing your blood
down the drain because the ache of loss is debilitating
and the devil inside you wants you to pay for the sins
you did not commit!
How I hate to see you lost because the girl over there
has all you ever wanted and it eats you up in ways you
can't control or fathom to explain in words because the
words don't give credit to the horrifying feelings you
can feel deep down and you want to see etched in your
flesh.
This is not your fault my darling and you are stronger
than you could ever imagine.
I know you have the power to take back the control but
just like Dorothy it's a power you "had to learn for
yourself"....
But this isn't a fairy tail.
There is no wizard.
There is only you.
The great and powerful you.
Believe and you CAN make it.

Bright Colours

Tweezers in one hand and my thoughts in the other
Why am I doing this?
What will I accomplish from pulling my toenails out?
Obviously the answer is nothing but somehow I can't
help but do it and why?
Because my brain turns red...
Or bright blue...
Or orange!
A bright and uncomfortable colour that I can't sit with
and the only way to go back to the normal shade that
means I can function is to do this horrible thing.
I don't enjoy it.
But I don't enjoy a lot of things I have to do.
This disorder, so they tell me, is called dermatilomania
which is the urge to pick at your skin or nails
But not in the same way a fourteen year old bites the
loose skin around their fingers but in the way a butcher
slices his meat for market
This is not something I enjoy but something I have to
do.
Because, brains aren't meant to be bright colours....
They're meant to be functioning.
And I am not right now

Thank you for reading

Please, if you take just one thing from this book

Let it be

That you

Are not

Alone.....